Possession

Canada

D0436018

New York

Michigan Territory

Pennsylvania

Philadelphia
MARCH 13

Pittsburgh

NJ

MISSISSIPPI R.

MISSOURI R.

Illinois

Indiana

Ohio

MD

DE

Sauk Indians

OHIO R.

APPALACHIAN MTS.

Virginia

KANSAS R.

Independence
APRIL 28

St. Louis
MARCH 24

Kentucky

North
Carolina

Missouri

Tennessee

South
Carolina

Arkansas Territory

ARKANSAS R.

Mississippi

Georgia

Alabama

Florida Territory

Louisiana

Gulf of

Mexico

EL DORADO COUNTY LIBRARY

3 1738 00578 4366

Townsend's
Warbler

EL DORADO COUNTY LIBRARY
345 FAIR LANE
PLACERVILLE, CA 95667

Also by Paul Fleischman

Picture Books

Time Train
Shadow Play
Rondo in C
The Birthday Tree

Novels

The Borning Room
Saturnalia
Rear-View Mirrors
Path of the Pale Horse
The Half-A-Moon Inn

Short Story Collections

Coming-and-Going Men: Four Tales
Graven Images: Three Stories

Poetry

Joyful Noise: Poems for Two Voices
I Am Phoenix: Poems for Two Voices

PAUL FLEISCHMAN

❧

Townsend's Warbler

A Charlotte Zolotow Book

An Imprint of HarperCollins*Publishers*

EL DORADO COUNTY LIBRARY
345 FAIR LANE
PLACERVILLE, CA 95667

For their assistance with this book I would like to thank
the Academy of Natural Sciences in Philadelphia; Hartnell
College's Library in Salinas, California; and Vern Yadon
and Paul Finnegan of the Pacific Grove Museum of Natural History in Pacific Grove, California.

In quoting from Townsend's writings, I have modernized
spelling and streamlined punctuation.

Paul Fleischman

Townsend's Warbler
Copyright © 1992 by Paul Fleischman
All rights reserved. No part of this book may be used or reproduced
in any manner whatsoever without written permission except in the
case of brief quotations embodied in critical articles and reviews.
Printed in the United States of America. For information address
HarperCollins Children's Books, a division of HarperCollins
Publishers, 10 East 53rd Street, New York, NY 10022.

Library of Congress Cataloging-in-Publication Data
Fleischman, Paul.
  Townsend's warbler / by Paul Fleischman.
    p.   cm.
  "A Charlotte Zolotow book."
  Summary: An account of the 1834 cross-continental journey of
naturalist John Townsend and his many discoveries, including the
warbler that bears his name.
  ISBN 0-06-021874-6. — ISBN 0-06-021875-4 (lib. bdg.)
  1. Townsend, John Kirk, 1809–1851—Juvenile literature.
2. Naturalists—United States—Biography—Juvenile literature.
3. Overland journeys to the Pacific—Juvenile literature.   4. Townsend's
warbler—Juvenile literature.   [1. Townsend, John Kirk, 1809–1851.
2. Naturalists. 3. Overland journeys to the Pacific. 4. Townsend's
warbler.]   I. Title.
QH31.T67F57   1992   91-26836
508.73'092—dc20   CIP
[B]   AC

Map Endpapers by Robert Romagnoli.
Typography by Anahid Hamparian
1   2   3   4   5   6   7   8   9   10
First Edition

To Betty and Mike Mojica

The Platte River by Albert Bierstadt.
Private Collection

~ 1 ~

DEPARTURES

On the morning of March 13, 1834, a coach clattered out of the great city of Philadelphia, bound for Pittsburgh. Inside it sat John Kirk Townsend and Thomas Nuttall. Winter was just giving way to spring, and the two were in high spirits. They were headed west, the compass setting they planned to keep for many months, leading them through lands with undiscovered plants, strange birds, new beasts. For they intended not to stop at Pittsburgh but to proceed down the Ohio River and cross the Mississippi, the Great Plains, the Rocky Mountains—to cross the entire United States all the way to the Pacific— and to be the first trained naturalists to do so.

Several thousand miles away, in the moun-

1

tains of Central America, a different group of travelers had also noted the change in seasons. Their journey would likewise be long, more than 3,500 miles, to the spruce and fir forests of the Pacific Northwest. Unlike Townsend and Nuttall, they would travel mainly by night, and by air. They were birds: small, their beaks short and sharp for plucking insects off leaves and branches, their feathers olive, deep black, and bright yellow. Restlessly flitting about the forests, they darted from limb to limb, hunting food, seeming never to remain still. They were not to be found in the books Townsend and Nuttall had studied. For despite the fact that their kind had flown this route each spring and fall for centuries, their existence was unknown to science. Very soon now they too would depart.

In Pittsburgh, Townsend and Nuttall booked passage down the Ohio River on the steamboat *Boston*. The hills of Pennsylvania, Townsend's home state, gradually disappeared behind him. He was twenty-four years old, handsome, upright, and well educated. A doctor whose real love was birds, he was a painstaking observer and skilled taxidermist who'd gained renown at an early age by discovering a new finch. With a cousin, he'd assembled a nearly complete collection of the birds of West Chester, Pennsylvania. Never before, however, had he ventured west of the Appalachians.

Nuttall, by contrast, had journeyed down the Ohio several times. Twice Townsend's age, gray haired and stout, he was one of North America's most-traveled men. Born in England, he'd been trained as a printer. Like Townsend, he'd abandoned his career in favor of his passion—in Nuttall's case, plants. At the age of twenty-two he'd come to Philadelphia and had set off plant collecting the very day after landing. In the course of twenty years of exploring, from the Great Lakes and the upper Missouri River to the Arkansas River and the swamps of Florida, he'd encountered

John Kirk Townsend,
Physician and Naturalist.
Courtesy of the Oregon
Historical Society

Thomas Nuttall, Naturalist.
Courtesy of the Harvard University
Art Portrait Collection, Harvard
University, Cambridge, MA. Gift of
Professor Edward Tuckermann
through Dr. Asa Gray for the
Gray Herbarium

quicksand, hostile tribes, swarms of insects, and river pirates. He'd nearly starved to death, almost been struck by lightning, become lost on the prairie, suffered through malaria, and even had Indians rummage through his collections and drink off the alcohol used to preserve animal specimens.

In spite of which, when his friend, the trader-adventurer Nathaniel Wyeth, invited him to join his expedition to the Oregon Country, Nuttall accepted at once. Here was a chance to roam west of the Rockies, to see plants no botanist had ever set eyes on!

Knowing he'd be gone for several years, he resigned his teaching position at Harvard. Knowing, too, that the trip would be dangerous, and perhaps fearing that he might not return, he gave many of his plants to a museum. A studious man, shy except with those who shared his devotion to nature, he'd met Townsend recently, been impressed with him, and invited him along.

On March 24 the *Boston* docked in St.

Louis. The naturalists bought clothes for the journey ahead: leather pants, bulky overcoats, and hats that seemed stiff enough to stop bullets. Townsend, a "greenhorn" new to the West, gawked at the sight of some Sac Indians—naked to the waist, tomahawks in their hands, their shaved heads painted in stripes of red and black. "I feel very much interested in them," he recorded in his journal, "as they are the first Indians I have ever seen who appear to be in a state of uncultivated nature." Fascinated, he filled several pages with notes on their dress and method of painting themselves.

With Nuttall, he set off on foot for Independence, Missouri, where they would meet up with Wyeth's party. The two were thrilled by enormous flocks of cranes and the sight of golden plovers covering the plains for acres. Missouri was the westernmost state in the Union, and settlements began to thin out. They were leaving civilization behind. Suddenly apprehensive of what lay ahead, Townsend heard a church bell toll and won-

Massika, Sauk Man by Karl Bodmer.
Courtesy of the Joslyn Art Museum, Omaha, NB

dered if he would ever hear another. "I was on my way to a far, far country," he wrote, "and I did not know that I should ever be permitted to revisit my own."

The men reached Independence and joined Wyeth's brigade. On April 28 the caravan of 70 men and 250 horses started west for Fort Vancouver, an outpost of the British Hudson's Bay Company 2,000 miles away on the Columbia River in the Oregon Country. "As we rode out from the encampment, our horses prancing and neighing and pawing the ground, it was altogether so exciting that I could scarcely contain myself," wrote Townsend. "Uproarious bursts of merriment and gay and lively songs were constantly echoing along the line."

Lewis and Clark had been the first to travel overland to the Columbia thirty years earlier. West of the Louisiana Purchase, the Oregon Country was claimed by both the United States and Great Britain. It was a vast area sparsely populated by Indians, a few mountain men, and the beavers they trapped, whose fur was in great demand as a material for hats. In 1811 the millionaire John Jacob Astor had financed an expedition in hopes of capturing the fur trade from the Hudson's Bay Company, but his post at Astoria, at the mouth of the Columbia, had fallen to the British in the War of 1812.

Those traveling the Oregon Trail with Wyeth had a variety of motives for journeying so far. Wyeth and his contingent of trappers hoped to take some of the fur trade from the British, enriching themselves and bolstering America's claim to the region. A party of Methodist missionaries had joined them, bound west to convert the Flathead Indians. For Townsend and Nuttall, the lure wasn't money or territory or souls, but flowering plants and flitting birds they'd never sniffed, seen, or dreamed of.

They'd hardly set off before Nuttall shot a new sparrow and Townsend a new species of longspur. These men weren't simply observers,

Trappers by Alfred Jacob Miller.
Courtesy of the Walters Art Gallery, Baltimore, MD

but scientists who needed to describe their finds minutely and bring back specimens for museums. In order to do as little damage to the bird skins as possible, they used very small shot and little gunpowder. Both men were crack shots and usually spent their evenings writing up notes and skinning and stuffing the specimens their guns had brought down during the day.

Following the Kansas River, they awoke to the singing of thrushes and buntings. The party met white wolves and herds of antelope. It also met the Great Plains' violent weather. A day-long downpour drenched the men and their bedding, and was followed by a hailstorm. "It came on very suddenly," wrote Townsend, "and the stones, as large as musket balls, dashing upon our horses, created such a panic among them that they plunged and kicked and many of them threw their loads and fled wildly over the plain." The men no longer bubbled with jests and song. One morning they discovered that the cook had left. A few days later three more men deserted.

They neared Pawnee country and feared meeting a war party. On an earlier trip, when weapons were being checked, Nuttall's gun barrel had been found to be clogged with dirt—he'd been using it to dig up plants. Here he could take no such chances. Each evening a watch was set up, any member of which who fell asleep would have to walk, rather than ride, for three days. The two naturalists served at night with the others, fighting sleep and calling out "All's well" to the next man every quarter hour. In the morning they breakfasted on bacon, dumplings, and coffee, broke camp, and pushed on another twenty miles or so before dark.

Wyeth's men swore at the scorching sun. The missionaries complained about the others' foul language. Pack horses lost their footing and plunged into the water while fording streams. One night while Townsend was serving on the watch, half the horses suddenly bolted from the camp. Riding the pitch-dark prairie, he followed them by the sound of their hoofs and managed to drive them back.

Finally, on May 18, the party arrived at the banks of the Platte River. "A mile wide and an inch deep," as it was commonly described, this was the river they planned to follow for many days and hundreds of miles — the river that would lead them west into the as-yet-unglimpsable Rocky Mountains.

In mid-April small flocks of the unnamed bird began their yearly migration north. The striking black-and-yellow-headed males had recently begun to sing. For several days they and the olive-crowned females had been eating ravenously, storing fat to fuel their journey. All winter the dark highland forests of Mexico and Central America had been alive with them. Suddenly, in the space of a week or two, they were gone.

Northwestward through Mexico they flew, in groups of their own kind or in company with other birds. Like most migrants, they flew mainly at night, navigating by the stars and usually covering a hundred miles or more in one flight. At dawn they dropped down among the trees and shrubs, hungrily feeding on insects, continuing to move toward the north even while searching for food. As the day wore on they became less active, resting up in preparation for the coming night's flight.

North along the slopes of Mexico's Sierra Madre they flew, across the Conchos River, the Rio Grande, the Gila, the Colorado. Traveling in a broad belt, many were already 2,000 miles from their winter homes—with almost as far still to go to their breeding grounds. There, where insects are abundant in spring and summer, and where there are few all-year resident birds to compete with, they would find plenty of food for themselves and their young.

As May progressed, so did the birds, spread out from the Pacific to the Rockies. Many of them wouldn't finish the journey. Storms, lack of water, heat, and sheer exhaus-

tion took their toll, removing the flocks'
weaker members.

North through the Coast Range, the Cascades, the Sawtooth, the Wasatch, the Wind River ranges, they flew. At last they reached their nesting habitat: dense, pungent forests of towering spruce and fir trees. Each bird returning to roughly the area in which it had bred the year before, some ended their journeys in Washington, Idaho, Montana, or Wyoming. Many continued into British Columbia. Some flew on as far as the Yukon and Alaska. After traveling for a month or more, they'd finally arrived. It was now mid-May, and time for their most important activity: raising their young.

The Rocky Mountains, 1863, by Albert Bierstadt
The Metropolitan Museum of Art, Rogers Fund, 1907.

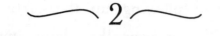

2

SUMMER, 1834

On May 19 the Wyeth expedition pushed westward alongside the Platte River. Townsend and Nuttall met sandhill cranes. The brigade also nearly met a war party of 1,500 Pawnees. Urging their packhorses to a brisk trot, the men rode until midnight, slept three hours, then rode hard all the next day to avoid them.

They entered the land of the buffalo. Topping a rise, they looked down on some eighty square miles of them. Buffalo meat at once became their staple, especially the tongue and hump, which were regarded as the tastiest parts. The expedition's hunters would pick a buffalo out of the herd and ride hard after it, the enormous animal tossing its head at the horses and plowing up the earth with its horns. Chased over the plains until it exhausted itself, the buffalo finally stopped, made a stand, and was shot at close range.

Anxious to pass the rite of killing his first buffalo, Townsend shot a large bull, only to find it had almost no meat on its bones. He laughed with the others at his inexperience. But in his journal he railed against unnecessary killing. "I have seen dozens of buffalo slaughtered merely for their tongues, or for practice with the rifle," he fumed. As for the killing of antelopes, "A number are however slaughtered every day from mere wantonness and love of killing, the greenhorns glorying in the sport like our striplings of the city in their annual murdering of robins and sparrows."

Spring was giving way to summer. The men were parched by the burning heat and suffered from intolerable thirst. Some sucked on musket balls or pebbles to stimulate saliva. Finding himself miles from water, Townsend became so thirsty that he thrust his head into a freshly killed buffalo and drank its heart blood with the other men.

The expedition turned up the North Fork of the Platte and was attacked by swarms of black gnats. The men pulled their coats over their heads and built fires in the mouths of their tents at night. The whole party's faces puffed up from bites. Wyeth's eyes swelled shut entirely, leaving him sightless for several days. Those who could open theirs had sand to contend with. "During the whole day a most terrific gale was blowing directly in our faces," Townsend reported. "Clouds of sand were driving and hurtling, and when we halted in the evening we could scarcely recognize each other's faces beneath their odious mask of dust and dirt."

Six of the men were suspected of planning to desert with their horses and had to be watched. The naturalists, however, were undiscouraged. Townsend added new birds to his collection. And Nuttall was exhilarated by the masses of bright-petaled prairie flowers.

"It was a most enchanting sight," wrote Townsend. "Even the men noticed it, and more than one of our matter-of-fact people exclaimed *beautiful, beautiful*. Mr. N. was here in his glory. He rode on ahead of the company and cleared the passages with a trembling hand, looking anxiously back at the approaching party, as though he feared it would come ere he had finished and tread his lovely prizes underfoot."

The naturalists' collections were overflowing their saddlebags. To make room for their specimens, they cast off spare clothing, soap, and anything else they could do without. Sunburned and whiskered like the others, a proven hunter and horseman, Townsend no longer stood out among Wyeth's men, and he looked with little regret on the luxuries ejected from his pack. "We are content to dress, as we live, in a style of primitive simplicity," he wrote. "Many of the men are dressed entirely in deerskins, without a single article of civilized manufacture about them."

One day a live specimen joined the party. A baby antelope, hardly larger than a kitten, was found along the way. The men fed him milk from a tin cup and named him Zip Coon. He soon became tame. Each morning, as if fearing to be left behind, the antelope bleated to be lifted into the willow basket in which he rode on the back of a mule.

Gradually the expedition had been gaining in altitude. On June 1 the men crossed the Laramie River and began climbing more steeply into the Rockies. The country was barren but for sagebrush. The air turned chill. The men shivered in their saddles. They passed Independence Rock, the "Register of the Desert," and read the list of previous travelers who'd carved their names into it. Following tradition, Wyeth, the party's leader, added his own.

Deeper into the mountains they rode. On June 10 they sighted the shimmering, snow-covered peaks of the Wind River Range. Nearer at hand Nuttall beheld a new whip-

Name carvings on Independence Rock, Wyoming.
© Bill and Jan Moeller; from their book *The Oregon Trail: A Photographic Journey*, 1985

poorwill, today known as Nuttall's poorwill.

Edible game, however, was in short supply, and some of the men began talking of eating Zip Coon. Nights grew colder. Kettles of water were found iced over in the morning. On June 14 they traversed South Pass, 7,550 feet. They were now west of the Continental Divide.

The brigade was nearing the annual rendezvous of Rocky Mountain trappers. There Wyeth hoped to trade for furs and give his horses a much-needed rest. On the way, in the course of fording a river, Townsend was

soaked to the neck by the ice-cold water—
then discovered to his horror that one of the
volumes of his journal, containing notes on
several new species of birds, had been swept
away by the current. He searched the river-
bank until dark and offered large rewards to
the men. The book was never found. Fortu-
nately, Nuttall had recorded in his own journal many of the descriptions Townsend had
lost.

After spending the day in damp clothes,
Townsend awoke the next morning feeling ill,
but had no choice but to ride with the others.

Nuttall's Whip-poor-will by John James Audubon.
From *The Art of Audubon: The Complete Birds and Mammals* by John James
Audubon, introduction by Roger Tony Peterson. © 1979 by Volair Lim-
ited. Reprinted by permission of Random House, Inc.

"I suffered intensely during this ride; every step of my horse seemed to increase it, and induced constant sickness and retching." When they halted at nightfall, Townsend had to be carried from his horse.

The brigade had reached the rendezvous on the lush banks of the Green River. Here the trappers sold their furs, bought supplies for the winter, and caroused. Confined to his tent, writhing with fever, Townsend was kept awake by the mountain men's whooping and fighting, the shouting of Indians, the barking of wolf-dogs, and the crack of rifles. Nuttall, meanwhile, studied in amazement the unfamiliar trees and flowers around him. "The botanist, in all this array, fails to recognize one solitary acquaintance of his former scenes," he wrote. "He is emphatically in a strange land."

After a two-week rest, the party broke camp on July 2. On the 4th Wyeth's men demanded the liquor kegs be opened in honor of Independence Day. "Slaves to Satan" the leader of the missionaries pronounced the men.

Detail from *Trappers' Rendezvous* by Alfred Jacob Miller.
Courtesy of the National Archives of Canada/Neg. no. C439

When a rifle salute was proposed, Townsend flattened himself on the ground as the lurching men discharged their guns in every direction.

Though the brigade celebrated America's independence, it was no longer in the United States. It had entered the disputed Oregon Country, and was only a few miles from the northern border of Mexican territory. It had also entered the domain of the most feared of all Indian tribes, the Blackfeet.

The caravan crawled through desolate, lava-covered hills. Mineral springs bubbled up beside the trail. One day a grizzly bear rushed upon the men, not falling until it had been struck by thirty bullets. That same evening the mule carrying Zip Coon caught its hoofs among the blocks of lava and fell, breaking one of the antelope's delicate legs. "From sheer mercy," lamented Townsend in his journal, "we ordered him killed."

The naturalists spotted a pair of birds named for two other travelers who'd passed this way: Lewis' woodpecker and Clark's nutcracker. They spied the Grand Tetons in the distance and worried with the others about the Blackfeet. "We have seen for several mornings past," Townsend noted, "the tracks of moccasins around our camp."

On July 13 they reached the Snake River, the great southern tributary of the Columbia. Here Wyeth decided to build a trading post. After three weeks of work, it was finished and given the name Fort Hall. On August 5 the American flag was raised over the fort, followed by another all-day drinking bout by Wyeth's men. "We had 'gouging,' biting, fisticuffing, and 'stamping' in the most 'scientific' perfection," wrote Townsend. "Such scenes I hope never to witness again; they are absolutely sickening, and cause us to look on our species with abhorrence and loathing."

The next morning the brigade began packing up. Twelve of Wyeth's men were assigned to the fort. To allow their slow-hoofed cattle a slower pace, the missionaries had set off ahead of the others, planning to rejoin them later.

Pioch-Kiäiu, Piegan Blackfeet Man by Karl Bodmer.
Courtesy of the Joslyn Art Museum, Omaha, NB

28

There were now only twenty-nine men in the party. Shortly before noon they left Fort Hall behind them and began the final—and the most difficult—leg of their journey.

Upon reaching their breeding areas in May, the male birds at once staked out territories. These would be their feeding grounds and would have to provide enough insects for themselves, their mates, and their hungry young. While other birds searched the forest's floor for food, or probed the trees' bark, or caught insects in midair, the unnamed birds hunted high in the treetops, where few other birds were to be found. Perched prominently within their territories, the males sang their thin, cheerful songs, punctuated by two high, clear notes at the end. Only the males sang, as is the case with nearly all birds. Echoing through the woods over and over, their songs announced that their treetops had been claimed, warning away other males of the same species. Their singing also advertised their availability to arriving females.

Soon the females had chosen their mates and decided on sites for their nests. Often these were a hundred feet up or higher, usually beneath protecting branches. While the birds and animals of the forest floor lived in perpetual twilight, it was much sunnier in the tops of the trees, where the females began building their nests. It was a task that required many trips, vertical and horizontal. Fir twigs, cedar bark, weed stems, pine needles, and grasses were gathered and woven together. Spider cocoons or tufts of elk or deer hair provided soft linings.

By the middle of June most nests contained four or five eggs, white with brown speckles. For the embryos to develop properly, the eggs had to be kept at an even, high temperature. This job of incubation too was performed by the females. Through the two weeks before their young hatched, the females sat on their eggs most of the day and night to keep them warm, leaving only to find food for themselves.

Though the eggs might have been laid over a period of days, they generally hatched within hours of each other. With its "egg tooth," a sharp protuberance on the beak, a hatchling poked a small hole through the shell, then turned around within the egg, sawing off the egg's cap and crawling out. The hatchlings' eyes were closed. They were unable to stand. Naked except for patches of down, the newborn birds could do little other than lift their heads and open their mouths for food.

The adult males, who'd been mere spectators until then, suddenly joined in bringing food to their young—a job too large for one bird. For the nestlings ate voraciously, growing quickly and keeping short the time during which they were vulnerable to predators. Both parents were kept busy providing them a generous, protein-rich diet of insects.

The young required protection as well as food. They had to be shielded from rain and cold until they were able to regulate their own temperatures. Each female, therefore, "brooded" her nestlings for several days, sitting on them to keep them warm, leaving them only to help catch insects. Within a few days, their eyes opened. They began flexing their muscles. They shed their soft down, replacing it with light-brown feathers.

Ten days or so after emerging from their eggs, the young birds were ready to fly and leave the nest. Like other birds, they weren't taught flying by their parents. They flew by instinct once their wing feathers had grown out sufficiently. Their first flights and first attempts at perching were often clumsy. Stumpy-tailed, still not full-grown, begging woefully for food, they continued to be fed by their parents outside their nests for several weeks.

While July passed, they practiced flying. They learned to listen to other birds' alarm notes, announcing a dangerous intruder. They learned to take cover when a hawk circled overhead. Their final accomplishment was learning to find their own food—to quickly comb the ends of branches for ants, beetles, leafhoppers, and other insects.

The adults raised only one brood. Once the young learned to feed themselves, their families disbanded. Nests, which birds use as cradles rather than houses, had been abandoned weeks before. The males sang much less now. Territories disappeared. Parents and young dispersed through the woods, often joining mixed flocks of other insect eaters.

In late summer the adult birds molted, replacing their worn and faded feathers with a new plumage, not as showy as that worn in the spring. The young acquired new feathers as well and now closely resembled their parents, sporting olive-and-yellow heads and pairs of white wing bars. It was on these fresh feathers that the birds took off in mid-August, the elder generations and the new, passing high above the Skeena River, the Fraser, the Columbia, and the Snake on their way south to their wintering grounds.

Mount Hood from the Dalles, 1871, by John Mix Stanley.
The University of Michigan Museum of Art.
Gift of Mrs. Edith Stanley Bayles and the late
Mrs. Jane C. Stanley, Acc. No. 1940.426

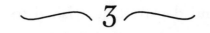

3

OREGON AND BEYOND

eading northwestward from Fort Hall, the Wyeth brigade entered a land without water, without shade, and without game. The horses' tongues hung from their mouths as they labored to haul the party's gear up rock-strewn passes and down sheer mountainsides. The men, baking in the furnacelike heat, sucked on stones to keep their mouths moist.

"One of our poor wearied horses gave up and stopped," Townsend recorded in his journal. "Kicking and cuffing and beating had no effect to make him move." The horse's pack was removed, and he was left where he lay.

The will to go on left the men as well. One man, raving from thirst, threw himself on the

35

ground and declared he wished to die there. Refusing to go further, he was left behind. When a pool of water was found that evening, he was brought to the camp and thrown in headfirst.

"We have no flour, nor vegetables of any kind, and our meat may be aptly compared to dry chips," Townsend wrote. When the party came upon an abundance of currants, the men feasted on them and only with difficulty were persuaded to push onward. A day later they ran out of food entirely, then chanced to shoot a stray buffalo. Whereas once they would have eaten the tongue and hump and left the rest to the wolves, this time they devoured everything but the bones.

Amid such hardship, the behavior of the naturalists must at times have irritated the others. After a day of inching over loose rocks at 10,000 feet, averting their eyes from the cliffs beside them, the men found that they'd followed a dead end and would have to retrace their way. Nuttall, however, was in high spirits: He'd found two new species of aster along the route. For such incomprehensible joy, the men of an earlier expedition had nicknamed him "the fool."

The party left buffalo country behind and entered the realm of the salmon. Meeting a band of Snake Indians, they happily traded with them at the rate of ten of the dried fish for one knife—a bargain tarnished by the severe stomach sickness that afflicted nearly all the men as a result of the change in diet.

On August 28 they crossed the Powder River. A few days later they lost their way among the mazelike Blue Mountains. The sky was filled with smoke, the sun hidden. Vast wildfires raged around them, hundreds of square miles in extent, blackening the grass that should have fed the party's horses. The men as well ran low on food. Returning to camp after a meager dinner of rose hips, Townsend discovered that the owl he'd shot that morning, a fine specimen he'd planned to preserve, was being eaten by two men—one of them the ravenous Nuttall.

On September 3 the expedition reached Fort Walla Walla and glimpsed the Columbia River at last. "I could scarcely repress a loud exclamation of delight and pleasure," Townsend wrote. "It is the noblest-looking river I have seen since leaving our Delaware."

Here they rejoined the missionaries, who set off down the Columbia in a barge. Townsend and Nuttall continued on horseback for five days, then boarded canoes to take them the rest of the way to Fort Vancouver. At once they were halted by a ferocious gale. The canoes were tossed violently about in the waves and rapidly took on water. Bailing for their lives, the men managed to reach shore—but not before Nuttall's huge plant collection was soaked. Townsend observed him hour after hour, sitting in front of an enormous fire "drying the papers, and rearranging the whole collection, specimen by specimen, while the great drops of perspiration roll unheeded from his brow."

The men proceeded, by canoe and on foot, drenched by a steady rain, wrapping themselves in soggy blankets at night. At eleven o'clock on the morning of September 16, the Wyeth expedition reached its destination, Fort Vancouver, and was welcomed by its British officers in spite of the Americans' status as rivals. By stagecoach, steamboat, horse, canoe, and foot, Townsend and Nuttall had journeyed more than 3,000 miles. Their travels, however, were still far from over.

Wyeth picked a site and began building his own trading post. The missionaries set off up the Willamette River and founded a mission. The naturalists, meanwhile, roamed the countryside, adding new plants, new animals, and many new shells to their collections. But they'd arrived too late to see the migration of birds heading south.

When the fall rains arrived, the pair decided to escape the wet winter months and take passage on Wyeth's brig, the *May Dacre*. The ship had brought supplies around Cape

Horn and was now bound for the Sandwich Islands—the future Hawaii. Setting off down the Columbia, Townsend and Nuttall passed the ruins of John Jacob Astor's fort and the site where Lewis and Clark had wintered. At the river's mouth they beheld, for the first time, the stormy Pacific.

"This is my first sea voyage," Townsend wrote in his journal, "and everything upon the great deep is of course novel and interesting to me." Land birds were replaced by gulls and petrels, herds of deer by schools of dolphins. After a three-week crossing the brig anchored off the island of Oahu, and the naturalists plunged into exploring the strange countryside.

Nuttall dug up five new species of shellfish in a single afternoon. Townsend was amazed by the bird life he saw. Both gaped at unfamiliar plants watered by 400 inches of rain a year.

They took great interest in the natives, jotting notes about their dress, their food, their grass houses. They dined on poi, the local sta-

ple. They met King Kamehameha III. After
several months, in March of 1835, they
boarded the *May Dacre* again, anxious to return with her to the Oregon Country as soon
as possible. They'd missed the previous autumn's migration of south-flying birds, scores
of species of which might be new to them.
This time they were determined to arrive in
time to meet them traveling north.

Like the naturalists, the unnamed birds
avoided winter by moving to a milder climate.
Lakes and ponds would be covered with the
lifeless bodies of insects after the fall's first
frost—and without insects the birds couldn't
survive. Leaving before snow and cold temperatures arrived, some passed the winter
along the Washington, Oregon, and California
coasts. The bulk of them, however, made the
much longer trip to Mexico and Central
America.

It was the first migration for the young
born that summer. They would take the place

Townsend's Warbler with young, near Leavenworth, central Washington State.
Photo © Bob and Elsie Boggs, 1962

of those older birds who'd died during the breeding season or in the course of the flight to the south. Spreading out among the mountains of Mexico, Honduras, Guatemala, and Nicaragua, most of the birds were returning to a region that was their home for more than half of the year.

Soon after the migrants arrived, the fall rains ended and the long dry season began. The land seemed aflutter with birds. Some were residents of the region all year long, the others coming from all parts of North America to escape the northern winter. Some kept to the warm lowlands, some to the hillsides higher up, while the unnamed birds chose the rugged mountains and deep valleys of the highlands. There, 5,000 to 10,000 feet up, so high that the forests stood among the clouds, they darted among the sharp-scented pines.

From September to April they wandered through the woods, twisting and turning down branches, plucking off insects, flashing the

Townsend's Warbler feeding.
Photo © Bob and Elsie Boggs, 1962

Breeding pair of Townsend's Warblers.
Photo © Bob and Elsie Boggs, 1962

white in their wings and tails as they flitted from tree to tree. Often they foraged with other birds. As the resident birds weren't breeding, most males weren't singing or chasing intruders, and the flocks were free to roam where they wished. The only sound they made was their constant *tsip*, a call announcing their presence in a tree, serving to keep the birds spaced apart while feeding.

As the days lengthened and spring arrived, new feathers grew in on their heads and throats. Each first-year male acquired the deep-black throat and brilliant yellow mask of his father.

Soon the birds' feeding call was joined by the sound of the males trying out their songs. For several days the birds gorged themselves on insects, building up food reserves. In the middle of April, in small detachments, they left on their journey far to the north, where the young would breed for the first time—a trip that would lead one of their kind into the annals of science.

Fort Vancouver, artist unknown.
Yale Collection of Western Americana, Beinecke Rare Book
and Manuscript Library, Yale University

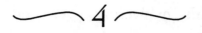

JOURNEYS' JUNCTURE

Three weeks after sailing from the Sandwich Islands, Townsend and Nuttall spotted auks bobbing beside the *May Dacre*'s bow. Soon after, they met vast flocks of geese and ducks and knew that land was near. On April 16 they dropped anchor in the waters of the Columbia.

The ship's cargo of cattle, sheep, and goats was unloaded. While Wyeth's men were busily preparing for the salmon season, the naturalists were equally busy: Spring flowers and spring birds had arrived. Here was the chance they'd been waiting for.

Setting out with rifle and game bag, Townsend found the forests ringing with songs he'd never heard before. Western birds

new to his marveling eyes and ears sur-
rounded him: singing, squabbling, building
nests, or restlessly foraging among the trees in
the midst of their migration farther north.
Catching sight of one, he raised his gun, took
careful aim, and fired.

The bird dropped through the air and
struck the forest floor. Catching up with it,
Townsend placed it on his palm. It was so tiny
as to feel nearly weightless. Its back was olive,
its wings gray. He counted white on six of its
tail feathers. Its head and throat were night
black, with a dawn-bright yellow mask cir-
cling its eye and reaching back to its shoulder.
The bird lay limp and warm in his hand. He
knew he'd never glimpsed its kind before, and
felt almost as if no other human had either. It
was a heart-spurring sensation.

"None but a naturalist," he wrote, "can ap-
preciate a naturalist's feeling—his delight
amounting to ecstasy—when a specimen such
as he has never before seen meets his eye."

Nuttall wrote down a few notes on the warbler his companion had shot. That fall he returned to the Sandwich Islands, then explored the coast of California, rounded Cape Horn, and sailed back to Boston, bearing hundreds of plant and animal specimens and many of the birds Townsend had shot. On November 15, 1836, an article describing some of those birds was read to the members of Philadelphia's Academy of Natural Sciences. It contained the first mention of the warbler Townsend had shot, a brief description based on Nuttall's notes and using the name Nuttall had conferred upon it—*Sylvia townsendi*, Townsend's warbler.

The following year the article was published, publicly registering the new bird's discovery. One of two specimens Townsend had shot was placed in the Academy's collection. It still serves as the "type specimen," the official representative of the species.

Townsend stayed on another year at Fort Vancouver, acting for a time as its doctor. He finally sailed home by way of the Sandwich Islands and Tahiti, arriving back in Philadelphia three and a half years after his departure. He found work as a museum curator and published the journal he'd kept during his trip. In 1844 the warbler bearing his name appeared in John James Audubon's *Birds of America*, painted from one of the specimens Townsend had shot. Married, father to a young son, he died prematurely at the age of forty-one, perhaps from constantly inhaling arsenic dust used in preparing birds for museum displays.

As for the route west that he and Nuttall traversed, it shortly became crowded with caravans of pioneers bound for the Oregon Country, and was soon known as the Oregon Trail. Wyeth's expedition, while a financial failure, was important in attracting the settlers whose numbers would win the region for the United States. In 1846 Great Britain signed a treaty accepting the forty-ninth parallel as the northern boundary of the United States west of Minnesota, bringing the future states of

Townsend's Wood-Warbler by John James Audubon.
From *The Art of Audubon: The Complete Birds and Mammals* by John James
Audubon, introduction by Roger Tony Peterson. © 1979 by Volair
Limited. Reprinted by permission of Random House, Inc.

Washington, Oregon, and Idaho, and parts of Montana and Wyoming, into U.S. territory.

For a century Townsend's warblers' preference for the treetops kept most facts about them unknown. Townsend met only migrating members of the species and was unable to learn anything about them. Comparatively little is known today. Only recently have ornithologists progressed beyond their forebear, Townsend, who wrote after his return from Oregon, "I procured but one specimen of this beautiful bird, on the Columbia River, in the spring of 1835. Early in the autumn of the same year, I shot another male, in a somewhat plainer livery. It does not breed here, and I know nothing of its habits."

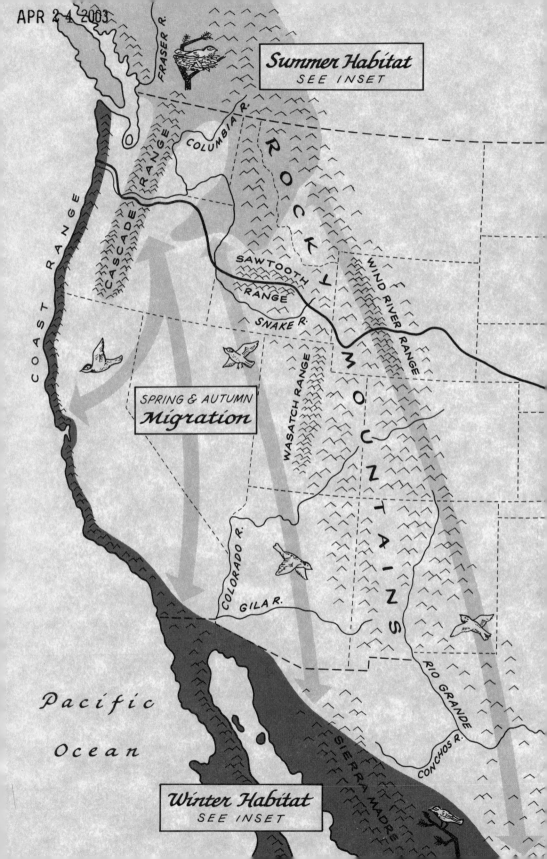

APR 2 4 2003

Summer Habitat
SEE INSET

FRASER R.

COLUMBIA R.

R O C K Y

CASCADE RANGE

COAST RANGE

SAWTOOTH RANGE

SNAKE R.

WIND RIVER RANGE

M O U N T A I N S

WASATCH RANGE

SPRING & AUTUMN
Migration

COLORADO R.

GILA R.

RIO GRANDE

CONCHOS R.

Pacific

Ocean

SIERRA MADRE

Winter Habitat
SEE INSET